# BLUE OCEAN STRATEGY CONCEPT

## Overview and Analysis

By Pierre Pichère

In collaboration with Brigitte Feys

Translation by Carly Probert

Management & Marketing    **50MINUTES**.com

# BLUE OCEAN STRATEGY

## KEY POINTS

- **Name:** Blue OceanStrategy
- **Uses:** Business, marketing and innovation
- **Why is it successful?** It beats the competition and guarantees performance
- **Key words:** Blue ocean, red ocean, strategy, innovation, creation of new strategic spaces, competition, business
  - ○ <u>W. Chan Kim</u> (born in 1952) is a member of the World Economic Forum in Davos and is considered by the Harvard Business Review to be one of the most influential thinkers in management and business. He co-directs the Blue Ocean Strategy Institute at INSEAD (European Institute of Business Administration) with Renée Mauborgne, where he also works as a professor.
  - ○ <u>Renée Mauborgne</u> (born in 1963) is a renowned professor of strategy and the co-director of the Blue Ocean Strategy Institute. In 2013, she was named one of the top five professors of MBA programs and received the C. Sloane prize a year later, awarded by the association of consultancy firms for excellence in research.

## INTRODUCTION

In today's fast-moving international business environment, creativity is becoming the key to long term performance. The need for new perspectives in innovation policies leads to groundbreaking ideas. Blue ocean strategy illustrates this perfectly.

## History

This strategy, released in 2005 by W. Chan Kim and Renée Mauborgne in the publication Blue Ocean Strategy: How to Create Uncontested Market Space and Make the Competition Irrelevant (translated into 43 different languages with 3.5 million copies sold worldwide), turns the theoretical foundations of strategic business innovation upside down. It encourages all economic stakeholders to do the same – with creative innovations called 'disruptives' – by investing in technology, conquering new markets or even collaborating with other social-economic stakeholders.

This strategy comes from a series of studies and is consistent with a number of other pieces of research, particularly those of the architect Clayton Christensen (born in 1952) and the director of Deloitte, Michael Raynor (born in 1967). It suggests a number of tools to create a systematic process of innovation.

The Blue Ocean Strategy Institute was opened in 2007, at the Fontainebleu campus of INSEAD, to examine the concept in more depth. The two authors have been awarded countless prizes and earned international recognition in both the business sphere and the world of marketing.

## Definition of the Model

The Blue Ocean model redefines the classic system of development strategies. Igor Ansoff (1918-2002), in one of his first publications that deals with business strategy, Corporate Strategy (1965), and even Michael E. Porter (born in 1947) with his five forces model for competition and value chains, both support this rethinking of business strategy. Their models are still used today in a number of sectors.

W. Chan Kim and Renée Mauborgne identify two types of markets in which economic stakeholders operate:

- The markets referred to as 'red oceans' represent saturated markets. Opportunity for growth is rare because so many stakeholders are involved, fiercely battling to widen their share of the market. The color red refers to the competition, but also to the suppliers, customers and purchasing advisers who want to maximize their own margins and shares of the market or other profitability measures (often involving outsourcing, merges, bankruptcy, etc.);

- The markets referred to as 'blue oceans' represent new domains where businesses can develop alone, with very little (or no) competition, thanks to radical innovation. This concept changes the structure of the market by creating an infinite amount (or 'ocean') of new demand. This is called 'value innovation' by the authors or 'useful innovation' on a wider scale.

Clearly distinguishing itself from classic central approaches towards differentiation through quality, cost leadership or even concentration, blue ocean strategy encourages businesses to break free from existing parameters in terms of supply and demand. Companies should explore other environments where they can add new value and gain a leading position.

# THEORY OF THE CONCEPT

By differentiating between red oceans and blue oceans, W. Chan Kim and Renée Mauborgne propose an analysis involving strategy, marketing and innovation.

## RED OCEANS VS. BLUE OCEANS

Based on marketing, analyzing the life cycle of a product is a classic method: after the launch comes growth, followed by maturity and then decline. This reasoning takes into account the volume of sales and the lifespan of the product (the quicker the speed of innovation, the shorter the life cycle of the product).

But what happens to the current and potential profitability? This depends on the competition, which determines prices, but also on the ability of the business to manage its own cost prices and develop penetration strategies, ensuring strong market coverage. A product still in its 'growing phase' is often marketed by numerous sellers. That's when the race to cut prices begins. This is precisely what W. Chan Kim and Renée Mauborgne call a 'red ocean' - a well-known strategic space where stakeholders recognize parameters, and inside of which they compete fiercely against each other. It is already clear that a simple application of this type leads to strategic choices regarding product range and financial equilibrium in terms of short, medium and long term profitability and growth.

Red oceans are increasing in the modern economical context and the majority of products are positioned in ripe markets. Moreover, the international opening of nearly every market stimulates the multiplication of stakeholders, which involves some competition, and is hardly compensated by the appearance of new economic sectors caused by technological progress. W. Chan Kim and Renée Mauborgne highlight how the traditional theory of business helps decision-makers to survive in a red ocean: concentration on the core business, outsourcing in order to lower cost prices, etc.

Blue ocean strategy invites stakeholders to abandon the red oceans, which are hardly creators of value, to move towards blue oceans. In these new strategic spaces, every business can evolve alone and, for a time, won't be subject to excessive constraints of competition and price wars.

**Value creation**

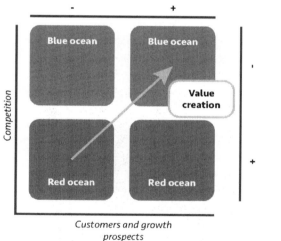

*Customers and growth prospects*

# SWITCHING OCEANS USING VALUE INNOVATION

The key to moving from a red ocean to a blue ocean is innovation. But innovation based purely on technology isn't enough. W. Chan Kim and Renée Mauborgne named the process of radical division that leads to a blue ocean 'value innovation'. This concept works for businesses in search of economic performance and customer satisfaction.

Without a doubt, the innovation described by the two authors requires nothing from economic stakeholders and calls itself a traditional neo-classic approach, considering innovation to be external. It's a voluntary business approach, where a reexamination of approach is needed for a successful transition. In this respect, it is driven by the economic stakeholders themselves. This type of innovation goes all the way back to Jean-Baptiste Say (journalist and economist, 1767-1832) and continues today through a variety of economists with very different ideas, such as Karl Marx (1818-1883) and Joseph Schumpeter (1883-1950).

The name 'value innovation' reflects the purpose of the blue ocean: to create more value, both for consumers, which will also attract new ones, and for the business, where pricing structures will be redefined in-depth with the aim of shifting market parameters.

## REEXAMINING EVERYTHING

Developing a blue ocean strategy requires a reexamination of framework assumptions made by markets, which market studies investigate by analyzing the existing structure.

- If a product is bought mainly by men, how can it be made interesting to women?
- If it is distributed exclusively through professional middlemen, is it possible to target the final customer directly?
- If it is intended for experts, is there a way to popularize it?

In this case, innovation does not mean high prices – which is often the case with innovations based on technology. Repositioning a product on the market by widening its audience can lead to an increase in the number of units sold, which then lowers the price by dividing the fixed costs. Also, rethinking uses can allow for the removal of some options or features that were deemed essential beforehand, reducing the final price. However, blue ocean strategy does not automatically lead to a reduction of prices, even if this is often the case. As an example, think about how PCs are replacing the mainframes of yesterday, or even how our smartphones have become substitutes for fixed telephones.

## EXCLUDING, REINFORCING, REDUCING AND CREATING

If blue ocean strategy involves 'moving the marker', once the parameters of a market in which a business develops are defined, it is still necessary to determine what needs to be reinforced, what needs to be reduced, what needs to be excluded and finally, what needs to be created (although this last factor was not initially included in the list).

This approach can be illustrated with an example from the automobile industry. In 1998, Louis Schweitzer, then owner of Renault, announced a radical innovation for the automobile market: a low cost car. This venture led to the creation of the Logan model. Initially intended for markets in Eastern Europe, the vehicle was also successful in France, which became the first country to import the Logan, manufactured in Romanian Dacia factories.

This success came from a strategy for redefining the model. Generally speaking, the automobile industry was a race towards the 'best': bigger vehicles, more comfort, more secure, more features, and, therefore, more expensive. By optimizing the similarities with different vehicles in the Dacia factories purchased in 1999 and rejecting the idea of a luxury vehicle, Renault discovered the secret to success. The Logan was marketed for 4,500 euros in emerging economies and 7,500 euros in France, where consumers required only basic features.

But low cost doesn't mean low quality. Although it doesn't have a walnut dashboard, the Logan is extremely robust as it targets markets where the road conditions are often far from ideal or where vehicle maintenance is much less developed than in Western countries.

Likewise, Renault breaks away from the habits of other companies by not restricting their less expensive cars to small city models (like the Twingo from the 1990s or the Smart car). With the Logan, Renault offers a family car with plenty of space inside and a large trunk.

### Excluding, reinforcing, reducing and creating

| **Excluding** | **Reinforcing** |
|---|---|
| Luxury | Endurance Interior space |
| **Reducing** | **Creating** |
| Comfort | Low cost price segment |

Blue Ocean Strategy © 50MINUTES.com

By redefining their strategy, Renault attracted more customers that expected: in addition to reaching its target market in the emerging economies, the Logan was equally appealing to French consumers who, for budget reasons, were usually forced to resort to the second-hand market. The low cost car caught the attention of the market that did not necessarily pride itself on the vehicle aesthetics, but always aimed for a good balance between quality and price.

# LIMITS AND EXTENSIONS OF THE MODEL

The scientific rigor of blue ocean strategy seems questionable in some aspects. Would it not be better to put the successes of businesses into perspective? Other theories are also applicable for understanding business conquer strategies. For example, the celebrated works of Thomas J. Peters, In Search of Excellence (1982).

## BLUE OCEAN STRATEGY – A GUIDE RATHER THAN A REVOLUTIONARY METHOD?

The success of the blue ocean strategy book is not without its critics. The publication offers an abundance of examples taken from every sector of the economy, making it easy to read, but some say this diversity of references shows a weakness in the theory. Others also highlight the deductive character of the approach upheld by W. Chan Kim and Renée Mauborgne. They achieved many great successes and created a concept that included all of them. Blue ocean strategy would be advantageous read in retrospect rather than using it as an innovative and effective method to develop a creative approach to the market, even though the authors provide their recommended steps for passing from one ocean to the other. Can every business success be interpreted as a use, conscious or not, of blue ocean strategy? The examples provided in the economics book, ranging from Henry Ford (American manufacturer, 1863-1947) to Guy Laliberté (founder of Cirque du Soleil, born in 1959), seem to lead to that conclusion, since people have practiced this method in the past without knowing it.

From a social science point of view, the lack of similarities in the examples is clear, which leaves the comparisons given by the scientific publication questionable. Were the starting points for each of the different businesses used as examples similar? Also, the initial situation of a red ocean is not specified in the book because it doesn't have a name, relative or absolute. No description is given for the market stakeholders or the critics in terms of the competition that marks the entrance to a red ocean. Similarly, if the arrival in a blue ocean is hardly measurable, this can lead to a fatal result. Businesses may venture towards the unknown based on innovation choices without knowing that their ideas will be accepted (and therefore purchased) by consumers.

Value innovation, the heart of the strategy put forward by the authors, tries to introduce a new concept, but one that lacks definition. The examples themselves demonstrate this weakness. They are taken from marketing, packaging or publicity, sometimes from organizations and businesses and other times from technological innovation or even science. Value innovation therefore comes down to the balance between capital gain for the business and low prices for the customer. But is this the result of technological innovation or better marketing positioning? The magnitude of value innovation seems unclear and this concept could cover a revolution on a product level as well as the adoption of more effective communication with consumers.

The method itself could also raise concerns. Building on the thorough reading of the value curve, blue ocean strategy wouldn't allow for breakthrough innovation, but lead only to incremental innovation, meaning the improvement of products or processes that already exist. The approach of W. Chan Kim and Renée Mauborgne was, in fact, founded upon using what already exists to create something new, to bypass the current situation and achieve radical innovation. As we will see later on, the two authors inspire many existing clients and potential businesses to come up with something new to offer.

Certain innovations, mainly the more radical ones, arise from skepticism. In fact, innovation does not always get immediate approval from the public. In his criticism of blue ocean strategy, innovation consultant BenoîtSarazin (specialist in 'marketing the uncertain') recalls spending 15 years at Nestlé creating Nespresso and how Guy Laliberté did not experience immediate success from Cirque du Soleil. The method is not a systematic process for success.

## INNOVATION FOR THE ECONOMY AND FOR BUSINESS: RELATED MODELS

Although they intend to perfect the theory of innovation, W. Chan Kim and Renée Mauborgne find themselves in line with Joseph Schumpeter (1883-1950) as a source of creative destruction. This economist has tackled innovation in every aspect, as much in terms of business organization concerning work and production as with marketing opportunities for products. What comes from the research of a blue ocean if not the destruction of old, original markets (or at least their reduction) in favor of the newly created ones? In addition to the life cycle already mentioned, we can also look at the risk of cannibalization. As part of a marketing strategy for managing a product range, this can cause a reduction in sales of existing products or a reduction of market shares in all commercial sectors: it is essential to assess if the profit generated by the new product will be greater than the potential losses of existing products. The business is essentially in competition with itself. However, this cannibalization can turn out to be a good strategy for an extension to a brand (for example, Marlboro) as long as it can afford entrance into a market that has so far been untapped by business. In this case, we catch a glimpse of the potential of the blue ocean.

The concepts of red oceans and blue oceans prompt the consideration of supported and breakthrough innovations put forward by

Michael E. Raynor and Clayton M. Christensen in their first publication, The Innovator's Dilemma: When New Technologies Cause Great Firms To Fail (1997). According to them, supported innovations improve existing products and breakthrough innovations remove the competition, creating a new market. This approach lines up with that of blue ocean strategy. Supported innovation corresponds to efforts made by economic stakeholders to survive in a red ocean, whilst breakthrough innovation leads to positive consequences for businesses that have progressed to a blue ocean.

# APPLICATION

Blue ocean strategy is a strategic model involving several steps.

## ADVICE

### Six questions to move towards a blue ocean

W. Chan Kim and Renée Mauborgne identify six central questions linked to the creation of a blue ocean strategy.

- **What alternatives are there on the market?** This involves adopting a customer's point of view to determine the options available. Two different products, whose creators believe to be completely independent, can find themselves in competition depending on the purchasing intentions of the customer. Also, holidays and work on the house make up two unavoidable expenditures: the year that a family is refurbishing a floor in the house, they will definitely spend less on a summer vacation.
- **What are the interests of the groups available?** This question is intended to give priority to the concerns of different groups available. These normally come down to two things: price and performance.
- **How is the chain of buyers and users made up?** Some businesses sell directly to the users, others sell through middlemen. Breaking this chain could be the answer to reaching a blue ocean. This is what Nespresso did by not selling its coffee pods through traditional networks (large food retailers), but by establishing their own line of high end stores.
- **What are the products and complimentary services?** This question is important because it enables successful strategic sequencing by picturing the two things together. Apple's success back in 2000

was due to the recognition that content (mainly digital downloads) was a vital offering alongside their products (iPod, etc.).

- **What is the functional or emotional aim of the sector?** Revitalizing the value or even stripping a product of its overly symbolic charge is part of the effort required for a blue ocean. The most pertinent example of this is Nespresso, a company that was able to create a luxury image for its coffee pods.
- **What main trends determine consumer behavior?** The protection of the environment and the search for personal fulfillment make up the main trends of contemporary societies, which will definitely inspire the creation of products and services for a blue ocean.

## Stimulation and creativity: a 4-step path

W. Chan Kim and Renée Mauborgne also propose a method for applying blue ocean strategy in enterprise. They identify four key steps:

- **Visual awakening** with the design of the value curve. For every characteristic of the offer, the company plots its weak points and strong points according to the competition. This first step mainly serves to create a consensus where company teams come together, through representation and the need for change, to allow for value creation. This places the company alongside its competitors. Is the differentiation clear or non-existent? According to the path the two curves follow, the answer will be clear;
- **Visual exploration** involves looking at the foundations to assess the innovative potential for development. How can you have an impact on a market if you don't know its consumers? Regularly consulting clients is useful, but not sufficient. The client is not necessarily the user of the product. Blue ocean strategy seeks to widen the existing customer base, and also question unrelated clients to get to know their habits and expectations;

- **Visual strategy fairs**, organized between members of the company and external people (clients, target markets, partners, etc.), let you validate the importance of the offered criteria. The objective is to build a strategy based on things other than intuition and internal obstacles, such as a resistance to change;
- **Visual communication** happens once there is a defined strategy. The entire team should be associated with the revolution of the company. Just like the understanding of existing limits was visual through the value curve, this phase also calls for artwork. It helps to visualize the new objectives acquired by all, independently from the hierarchy level, from blue ocean strategy.

### Pioneer, mover and non-mover products

Among the many tools highlighted by W. Chan Kim and Renée Mauborgne, analyzing the products of the business has proven to be a useful tool for strategy building. The authors suggest that products can be sorted into three categories:
- **Non-movers** are the products in the standard industry sectors. These products or services conform to the most current value curve and their future prospects are very limited in our highly scalable markets. They belong to the red ocean;
- **Pioneers** are the products that create unprecedented value. Mass consumption and strong growth are expected in the coming years. They embody the blue ocean;
- **Movers** are products that alternate between the two previous categories. While improving value for the customer and the company, they are not innovative enough to stay permanently in the blue ocean.

## Types of product

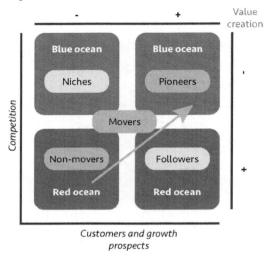

Blue Ocean Strategy © 50MINUTES.com

## Reaching new customers

The heart of blue ocean strategy attracting new customers. The survival techniques in a red ocean mean reducing the market shares of the competition. However, if we look at the transfer of customers from one stakeholder to the other, the size of the market remains unchanged. Blue ocean strategy seeks to expand the market by replacing its borders, thanks to the inclusion of customers from categories that, until now, did not purchase this type of goods.

There are three different types of non-customers:

- Soon-to-be non-customers occasionally purchase the goods or services offered by the company, but they are waiting for a better offer. There are many of them, but the market is fragile. This is the case of the British fast food chain Prêt à Manger that attracts a professional customer base that previously went to traditional restaurants as there was nothing better available;

- 'Refusing' non-customers, also known as 'dismissive non-customers' (Kotler (Philip) and Keller (Kevin Lane), Marketing Management, Paris, Pearson, 2006), never use the products or services of the studied market, perhaps because they are against it or because they cannot afford them. For example, the populations of urban cities are rising, to which very few 4×4 vehicles are sold since they are known to be more polluting and difficult to park in cities;
- 'Unexplored' non-customers are not fully involved in this market because the policy makers have never chosen to target them. They could also represent potential customers.

## CASE STUDY – THE WII, THE BLUE OCEAN OF NINTENDO

In 2006, Nintendo launched the Wii. This gaming console saw rapid growth that created considerable benefits for the company for a number of years. The sales of the console were very satisfactory, and it's the video game platform whose success is the most evident. Wii Sports has sold more than 80 million copies, a result that hugely surpassed those of competitors. Undoubtedly, Nintendo falls under the examples of blue ocean strategy for shaking up technology, but also for redefining pricing policies and the parameters of the market.

### The Wii according to the six questions of blue ocean strategy

- **What alternatives are there on the market?** Rather than positioning itself in relation to its competitors on the video game market, Nintendo is concerned with the hobbies of the population. In fact, since the development of artistic and creative practices, along with health and fitness making up two key bases since the 2000s, the firm decided to create its own market, associating its own expertise on gaming consoles with the development of new uses; sport (the Wii Sports game sold over 80 million copies), dancing, keeping fit, playing music, etc. All of these virtual activities are made possible with the Wii technology, which is based on the detection of movement instead of the traditional joystick.

- **What groups are available?** In terms of price, the Wii was positioned below its main competitors, who progressively had to compete. This strategy seeks to widen the video game audience, to one that's older and less attentive. The product, though innovative in its functionality, is less qualified in terms of some of its components in comparison to those of its competitors, the PS3 and the Xbox. This reduction of standards lowers prices by slightly limiting the technological possibilities, which are less important for a console created for all ages, with games that are less focused on speed and high resolution.

- **How is the chain of buyers and users made up?** A video game company since its establishment at the end of the 19th century, the company Nintendo has chosen to directly address its users, without using a middleman, in order to market the games available for the Wii. This type of evolution is now possible thanks to the generalization of the internet. In 2006, the same time as the revolutionary gaming launch, Nintendo also developed the Wii Shop alongside, which allowed users to earn loyalty points according to their gaming purchases.

- **What are the products and complimentary services?** Two complementary products have added to the launch of the Wii; the accessories and the games. The Wii mote, a remote control for the Wii, communicates with the console by Bluetooth. Equipped with an accelerometer, it transmits the movements of the player to the console: jumps, sideways movements, twists, etc. Later on, other accessories appeared, some of which have a microphone or even a drawing table, which allow users to adapt the console into a board game like Pictionary, targeting the family market. Nintendo has, of course, made sure that it markets the more popular Wii products such as Mario Bros. and Zelda. Finally, at the heart of its success, heart rate monitors and the Wii balance board, which recognizes foot movements, can transform the player's house into a gym, using the console as an instructor. It's half way between gaming and fitness.

- **What is the functional or emotional aim of the sector?** Video games aim to be both technological and cultural. The evolutions observed since the first console models, way back in the seventies, are both enormous and rapid. We must remember that the Wii has now been replaced by other products. The development is like that of computers, going from large central units to portable laptops to touch screen tablets. But the video game has also become a cultural problem: the first games, for example, many of which came from Nintendo have become references to generations that grew up in the eighties. The universe of Space Invader, Mario Bros. or Zelda, form part of a representative collection. The more contemporary games create communities of gamers that exchange information and form virtual relationships. Nintendo has to maintain this strong cultural dimension through their Wii games. That way, the people in their sixties don't become nostalgic and miss the world of Super Mario. To encourage them to become customers of a games console, you must offer alternative perspectives and use the functionality and technology to your advantage. The navigation and display on the Wii is considerably simplified, putting the user at ease that it is at a low enough level for their technological knowledge.
- **What main trends determine consumer behavior?** In the games offered for the Wii, Nintendo has captured the main trends in Western societies. The aging of society – more noticeable in Japan – has inspired the development of this console that is more universal than its competitors. The brain training program from Dr.

Kawashima (born in 1959) has also seen big success, particularly from the demand of older customers. Personal development and self expression through creativity are both strong aspirations in today's society. For a few years, the Wii has led the trend by proposing new products, sharing value with the customer – games that even allow users to keep fit physically and mentally – with low production costs. Nintendo has succeeded in generating profit thanks to the Wii, and not only with game sales but also since certain competitors have not had the same success, selling their consoles at a loss to catch up with the products and services on the rise.

## The Wii and its three types of non-customers

The success of the Wii provides an excellent analysis of non-customers who have moved the borders of the market. Nintendo had to accept the need to fight and keep a technological advantage or a price advantage. This would have allowed it to gain an advantage over market shares, but only temporarily as competitors replicate it so quickly. They have not given up fighting for non-customers (i.e. those who can pass from one supplier to another according to their offers).

Nintendo has succeeded in attracting the 'refusing' customers, even if, like the television years ago, the video game is a debated issue. They are accused of causing addiction among youths and encouraging extreme violence. It is often difficult to apply such critics to Wii Sports, which offers the possibility to practice tennis or bowling in your living room. Let's also remember that this game has sold 80 million units, making it the most bought video game in history, surpassing even Super Mario Bros. which has only sold 40 million units in comparison.

Finally, Nintendo has attracted the 'unexplored' customers, who have never explored the world of gaming. Not especially passionate about graphics or technology, adults, even the elderly, these users have found something in the Wii to relax and entertain them. This phenomenon would have seemed impossible a few years earlier.

In 2012, Nintendo tried to repeat its performance by launching the Wii U, hoping it would replace the Wii. Unfortunately, it seemed that the environment had evolved a lot in six years, particularly through the use of touch screen tablets and smartphones. Access to games was so generalized that people often dismissed the idea of consoles. This is the outcome of such an enthusiastic public. What does the future hold for this innovative company?

# SUMMARY

- Blue ocean strategy is a new model of economic governance towards performance.
- In a world that's getting more and more competitive, companies resort to taking market shares from under their competitors and the number of bankruptcies is rising.
- This innovative strategy, theorized by W. Chan Kim and Renée Mauborgne, professors at INSEAD, describes how businesses can free themselves from fierce competition in the 'red ocean' markets by finding 'blue ocean' markets where they can evolve alone (for a while).
- The metaphor of red oceans (sectors with strong competition) and blue oceans (niche markets with little competition) enable us to describe the market as a whole.
- Switching from a red ocean to a blue ocean is done through value innovation, which increases the use value for the customer and improves the economic model of the business. This could also lead to a lowering of sales prices.
- Blue ocean strategy is based on moving market parameters, questioning values and beliefs and attracting customers who weren't available on this market before, by changing the trends of positioning and distribution.
- In periods of financial uncertainty and major concerns about cost-cutting, you mustn't forget about the financial risks and techniques linked to the market. In fact, the human mind cannot forget what already exists to imagine what doesn't, such as radical new ideas that economists call breakthrough innovations. It is therefore impossible to predict how consumers will react.
- Finally, this approach calls for, according to its current context, the importance of innovation and the creation of markets.

Unfortunately, it doesn't always explain why few societies choose to use it. We cannot deny that the majority of businesses are limited with optimization of their existing products and/ or services.

# FURTHER READING

- Cazals (François), 'Stratégie Océan bleu de la Wii', in *Distriforce. Stratégies innovantes*, accessed 23rd May 2014. http://cazals.fr/strategie-ocean-bleu-de-la-wii/
- Kim (W. Chan) and Mauborgne (Renée), *Stratégie Océan bleu : comment créer de nouveaux espaces stratégiques*, Paris, Pearson, coll. Village mondial, 2010.
- Kotler (Philip) and Keller (Kevin Lane), Paris, Pearson, *Marketing Management*, 2006.
- 'Océans bleux et océan rouges', in *Démeter et Kotler*, 2012, accessed 23rd May 2014. http://demeteretkotler.com/2012/07/11/ocean-bleu-ocean-rouge/
- *Portail de l'INSEAD* (Blue Ocean Strategy Institute), accessed 9th May 2014. http://www.insead.edu/blueoceanstrategyinstitute/home/index.cfm
- Sarazin (Benoît), 'Pourquoi la méthode Blue Ocean ne suffit pas', in *Le blog de l'innovation de rupture*, accessed 23rd May 2014. http://benoitsarazin.com/francais/2013/10/methode-blue-ocean-suffit-pas.html
- 'Stratégie Océan bleu', in *Des Livres pour changer la vie*, accessed 23rd May 2014. http://www.des-livres-pour-changer-de-vie.fr/strategie-ocean-bleu/
- Tabatoni (Pierre), *Innovation, désordre, progrès*, Paris, Economica, 2005.
- Timos (Laurent), Ghoggal (Maxime) and Poubady (Barath), *Mercatique de la Wii*, accessed 23rd May 2014. http://laurent-timos.olympe.in/communication/Dossier%20Mercatique%20Nintendo%20Wii.pdf

# PROPEL
## YOUR BUSINESS FORWARD!

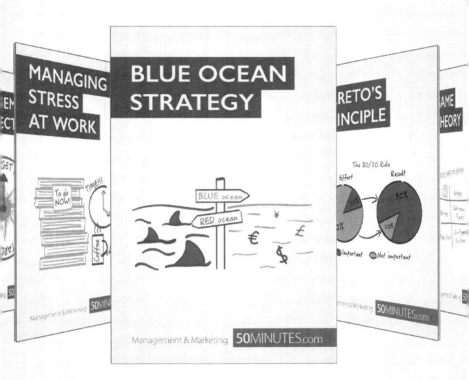

## Find out more on
## www.50minutes.com

www.50minutes.com

Publisher: Lemaitre Publishing
Rue Lemaitre 6 | BE-5000 Namur
info@lemaitre-editions.com

ISBN ebook: 978-2-8062-6466-4
Paper ISBN: 978-2-8062-6467-1
Cover photo: © Lisiane Detaille

Digital conception: **Primento**,
the digital partner of publishers.

Made in the USA
Lexington, KY
14 May 2016